50 Signs of Writing Success

How to Know You've Really Made It

Scott Tilley

Tauhida Parveen

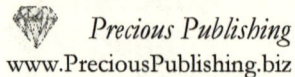

Precious Publishing
www.PreciousPublishing.biz

ISBN: 1503290786
ISBN-13: 978-1503290785

DEDICATION

To writers everywhere: stick with it, because nothing beats the writing life.

PREFACE

The writing life is a journey, one that is often lonely but always gratifying. Some writers are just starting out. Some writers have just published their first book. And some writers have just begun to experience the rich rewards that come from commercial and literary success.

There are certain characteristics that most writers share. For example, writers like to keep notes and story ideas on scrap pieces of papers all over the house – so much so that you begin to wonder if Post-It is your office wall's natural color. These and other telltale signs that you're a writer have been catalogued before.

But how do you know **you've made it** as a writer? What are the signs of success? And how do you know when you've *really* made it as a writer – someone who's reached the rarified heights of publishing success?

If you know what to look for, you can plan accordingly.

This book contains fifty signs of writing success. Each sign has two parts. The first part tells you that you've made it as a writer, but you're probably still at the early stages of your career. The second part tells you that you've really made it as a writer, because you've grown to appreciate the truths of modern publishing.

Hopefully, you'll recognize some of these signs in yourself. The signs are meant to be amusing and slightly tongue-in-cheek, but like all forms of humor they are based on observation and reality. Only a slight exaggeration is needed to make a point stronger.

Please feel free to contact us anytime. We can be reached via email at scott@stilley.org or online at http://www.facebook.com/stilley.writer .

Scott Tilley & Tauhida Parveen

November 2014

Melbourne, FL

50 Signs of Writing Success

How to Know You've Made It

You read your first harsh review in print. ☹

50 Signs of Writing Success

How to Know You've Really Made It

It doesn't bother you. ☺

50 Signs of Writing Success

How to Know You've Made It

You see your book advertised on Amazon.com. ☺

50 Signs of Writing Success

How to Know You've _{Really} Made It

But you don't buy yourself

another copy. 😐

50 Signs of Writing Success

How to Know You've Made It

Your friends and family ask how your latest book is coming along.

50 Signs of Writing Success

How to Know You've _{Really} Made It

How to Know You've ∧ Made It

You don't know which book they are asking about, since you're working on several at a time. ☺

50 Signs of Writing Success

How to Know You've Made It

You just signed a publishing contract. ☺

50 Signs of Writing Success

How to Know You've ∧ Really Made It

It's not your first. ☺

50 Signs of Writing Success

How to Know You've Made It

You received a rejection notice, but you'll keep trying. ☹

50 Signs of Writing Success

How to Know You've _{Really} Made It

Besides, you have multiple

offers from other publishers.

50 Signs of Writing Success

How to Know You've Made It

You've been asked
to critique someone
else's work. ☺

50 Signs of Writing Success

How to Know You've _{Really} Made It

How to Know You've ^Really^ Made It

But you don't have time. ☹

50 Signs of Writing Success

How to Know You've Made It

You give your books
as gifts. ☺

50 Signs of Writing Success

Really
How to Know You've ∧ Made It

Someone besides your mom

actually likes them. ☺

50 Signs of Writing Success

How to Know You've Made It

Your business card says "Writer." ☺

50 Signs of Writing Success

How to Know You've _{Really} Made It

So does your tax return. ☺

50 Signs of Writing Success

How to Know You've Made It

You use Facebook and Twitter. ☺

50 Signs of Writing Success

How to Know You've ∧ Made It
Really

But only to publicize your

own work. ☺

50 Signs of Writing Success

How to Know You've Made It

You've framed your
first royalty
cheque. ☺

50 Signs of Writing Success

How to Know You've ∧ Made It
_{Really}

The rest went straight into

the bank. ☺

50 Signs of Writing Success

How to Know You've Made It

You go to a lot of writers' conferences. ☺

50 Signs of Writing Success

How to Know You've ^{Really} Made It

But only to speak. ☺

50 Signs of Writing Success

How to Know You've Made It

You worry about people stealing your work. ☹

50 Signs of Writing Success

Really

How to Know You've ∧ Made It

Because they've already
posted illegal copies of your
previous books online. ☹

50 Signs of Writing Success

How to Know You've Made It

You write what you want, not what's hot.

50 Signs of Writing Success

Really

How to Know You've ∧ Made It

You know "cream will float,

but shit will sell." ☺

"New Babies; New Toys" by Andy McCluskey and Paul Humphreys of *Orchestral Maneuvers in the Dark* (OMD), from the album "History of Modern," 2011.

50 Signs of Writing Success

How to Know You've Made It

Other writers ask for your agent's contact information. ☺

50 Signs of Writing Success

How to Know You've ^{Really} Made It

How to Know You've ^ Made It

What agent? ☺

50 Signs of Writing Success

How to Know You've Made It

Your work is translated into other languages for sales worldwide. ☺

50 Signs of Writing Success

How to Know You've _{Really} Made It

Your overseas market is

larger than your domestic

one. ☺

50 Signs of Writing Success

How to Know You've Made It

Your books are available in audio format. ☺

50 Signs of Writing Success

How to Know You've ∧ Made It
Really

You do the narrating. ☺

50 Signs of Writing Success

How to Know You've Made It

People are starting
to recognize your
name as a writer.

50 Signs of Writing Success

How to Know You've ^{Really} Made It

Your next novel will be

published under a

pseudonym. ☺

50 Signs of Writing Success

How to Know You've Made It

You have a favorite spot in the house to do your writing.

50 Signs of Writing Success

Really
How to Know You've ∧ Made It

You have several houses to

choose from. ☺

50 Signs of Writing Success

How to Know You've Made It

You have been
commissioned to
write a screenplay.

50 Signs of Writing Success

How to Know You've _{Really} Made It

It's based on your own book.

50 Signs of Writing Success

How to Know You've Made It

You get asked to speak on a cruise.

50 Signs of Writing Success

How to Know You've _{Really} Made It

You use the cruise to write

your next novel. ☺

50 Signs of Writing Success

How to Know You've Made It

You only write if
you get paid. ☺

50 Signs of Writing Success

Really
How to Know You've ^ Made It

Unless you're an academic.

50 Signs of Writing Success

How to Know You've Made It

You have your own
.com domain. ☺

50 Signs of Writing Success

How to Know You've ∧ Made It
Really

You have ads on your website

— and they make money. ☺

50 Signs of Writing Success

How to Know You've Made It

You dress like your favorite writer. ☺

50 Signs of Writing Success

How to Know You've _{Really} Made It

People start to imitate you.

50 Signs of Writing Success

How to Know You've Made It

You have a thesaurus in every room in your house.

50 Signs of Writing Success

How to Know You've ^{Really} Made It

But your vocabulary is so

impressive you never use

them. ☺

50 Signs of Writing Success

How to Know You've Made It

You find your book
in the stacks of
the local bookstore
or public library.

50 Signs of Writing Success

How to Know You've Really Made It

Your books are prominently displayed at the front of the store – and at the top of the search results pages of Amazon.com and Google. ☺

50 Signs of Writing Success

How to Know You've Made It

You've made a pilgrimage to Shakespeare's house in the UK.

50 Signs of Writing Success

How to Know You've ^{Really} Made It

How to Know You've ∧ Made It

You met with J.K. Rowling

while you were there. ☺

50 Signs of Writing Success

How to Know You've Made It

You've been to Hemingway's house in the Florida Keys. ☺

50 Signs of Writing Success

How to Know You've _{Really} Made It

How to Know You've ∧ Made It

You've had a sit down with

Stephen King in Maine. ☺

50 Signs of Writing Success

How to Know You've Made It

You've been on C-SPAN2's BookTV. ☺

50 Signs of Writing Success

How to Know You've ᴧ Made It
Really

You've also been on Oprah,

Ellen, and Today. ☺

50 Signs of Writing Success

How to Know You've Made It

You have a special fountain pen for autographing your books. ☺

50 Signs of Writing Success

How to Know You've _{Really} Made It

How to Know You've ∧ Made It

You also have a Sharpie for autographing other things – like body parts. ☺

50 Signs of Writing Success

How to Know You've Made It

You have an agent.

50 Signs of Writing Success

How to Know You've _{Really} Made It

You have your pick of agents

– but you don't need one. ☺

50 Signs of Writing Success

How to Know You've Made It

You're recognized
at the airport. ☺

50 Signs of Writing Success

How to Know You've _{Really} Made It

But you lie about who you

are so you don't have to talk

about yourself again. ☺

50 Signs of Writing Success

How to Know You've Made It

You've finally been asked the question, "Where do you get your ideas from?" ☺

50 Signs of Writing Success

Really
How to Know You've ∧ Made It

You can actually answer. ☺

50 Signs of Writing Success

How to Know You've Made It

You understand how Microsoft Word's figure placement works. ☺

50 Signs of Writing Success

Really

How to Know You've ∧ Made It

You have people for that. ☺

50 Signs of Writing Success

How to Know You've Made It

You no longer suffer from writer's block. ☺

50 Signs of Writing Success

How to Know You've ^{Really} Made It

You never miss deadlines;

what's "writer's block" ? ☺

50 Signs of Writing Success

How to Know You've Made It

You write a blog that has a lot of traffic. ☺

50 Signs of Writing Success

How to Know You've _{Really} Made It

How to Know You've ^Really Made It

You don't waste your time

blogging. 😐

50 Signs of Writing Success

How to Know You've Made It

You're not a good public speaker but you're still asked to talk about your books at events. ☺

50 Signs of Writing Success

How to Know You've ⌃ Made It
Really

You're a great orator and a
wonderful storyteller. ☺

50 Signs of Writing Success

How to Know You've Made It

Everyone wants to tell you their story. ☺

50 Signs of Writing Success

How to Know You've _{Really} Made It

All you can think about while they are talking is how to use their story in your next book.

50 Signs of Writing Success

How to Know You've Made It

You get into arguments with your editor over sentence structure. ☹

50 Signs of Writing Success

How to Know You've _{Really} Made It

If it's good enough for

Cormack McCarthy, it's good

enough for you. ☺

50 Signs of Writing Success

How to Know You've Made It

You get into arguments with your copyeditor over punctuation. ☹

50 Signs of Writing Success

How to Know You've _{Really} Made It

If it's good enough for

William Faulkner, it's good

enough for you. ☺

50 Signs of Writing Success

How to Know You've Made It

You can really
relate to the movie
"The Words." ☺

50 Signs of Writing Success

How to Know You've _{Really} Made It

You understand copyrights, trademarks, and fair use. ☺

50 Signs of Writing Success

How to Know You've Made It

The movie "Authors Anonymous" reminds you of your past self.

50 Signs of Writing Success

How to Know You've _{Really} Made It

Because you've been

ambushed like publishing

agent David Kelleher. ☺

50 Signs of Writing Success

How to Know You've Made It

You've written your memoirs and they are selling. ☺

50 Signs of Writing Success

How to Know You've Really Made It

You've already signed a

contract for the next volume

in the series. ☺

50 Signs of Writing Success

How to Know You've Made It

You've created such popular characters that people start identifying with them. ☺

50 Signs of Writing Success

How to Know You've _{Really} Made It

How to Know You've ∧ Made It

You kill off the most popular

characters because you're

sick of writing about them.
😐

50 Signs of Writing Success

How to Know You've Made It

Your book has touched a nerve and causes a lot of dinnertime discussion. ☺

50 Signs of Writing Success

How to Know You've _{Really} Made It

How to Know You've ∧ Made It

Your book is banned. ☺

50 Signs of Writing Success

How to Know You've Made It

You have a big network of experts to use for background research on complex topics.

50 Signs of Writing Success

How to Know You've Really Made It

You can explain complex topics in a newspaper column of 500 words. ☺

50 Signs of Writing Success

How to Know You've Made It

Your characters are immoral and the plot is violent but people still want to read the story.

50 Signs of Writing Success

How to Know You've _{Really} Made It

Sesame Street does a parody skit about it. ☺

50 Signs of Writing Success

How to Know You've Made It

You can argue why "Fifty Shades of Grey" was poorly written. ☺

50 Signs of Writing Success

Really
How to Know You've ∧ Made It

You wish you wrote it. ☺

50 Signs of Writing Success

How to Know You've Made It

You write novels with complex immersive worlds that really draw people in. ☺

50 Signs of Writing Success

How to Know You've $\wedge$ Made It
Really

People believe your historical

fiction is historical fact. ☺

50 Signs of Writing Success

How to Know You've Made It

You can afford to spend three months a year in the Caribbean writing a novel. ☺

50 Signs of Writing Success

How to Know You've ⌃ Made It

Really

The movie based on your

book is already optioned

before you head home. ☺

50 Signs of Writing Success

How to Know You've Made It

You bought this
book. ☺

50 Signs of Writing Success

Really

How to Know You've ∧ Made It

Someone bought it for you.

50 Signs of Writing Success

ABOUT THE AUTHORS

Scott Tilley has published eight books, has authored over 100 academic papers, and writes the weekly "Technology Today" column for the *Florida Today* newspaper (Gannett). He is President of the Space Coast Writers' Guild and an ACM Distinguished Lecturer. He's also a Professor at the Florida Institute of Technology, where he is Director of Computing Education.

Tauhida Parveen is a writer, a software testing consultant and trainer, a group fitness instructor, and a REALTOR®. Her most recent book is *Software Testing in the Cloud: Migration & Execution* (Springer). She wrote the "Exercise for Busy People" column for the *Florida Today* newspaper (Gannett). She's on the ASTQB's Board of Directors. She's also Program Director of Software Engineering at Keiser University.

www.ingramcontent.com/pod-product-compliance
Lightning Source LLC
Chambersburg PA
CBHW050408290526
45786CB00003B/1176